stewarding
LIFE

one lifetime,
limited resources,
eternal priorities

Paul Chappell

Striving Together Publications
4020 E. Lancaster Blvd.
Lancaster, CA 93535
800.201.7748

Cover design by Andrew Jones
Layout by Craig Parker
Edited by Monica Bass and Joanne Bass
Special thanks to our proofreaders

The author and publication team have put forth every effort to give proper credit to quotes and thoughts that are not original with the author. It is not our intent to claim originality with any quote or thought that could not readily be tied to an original source.

ISBN 978-1-59894-252-1
Printed in the United States of America

Table of Contents

Stewarding Life

Text

GENESIS 1:26–28

26 And God said, Let us make man in our image, after our likeness: and let them have dominion over the fish of the sea, and over the fowl of the air, and over the cattle, and over all the earth, and over every creeping thing that creepeth upon the earth.

27 So God created man in his own image, in the image of God created he him; male and female created he them.

28 And God blessed them, and God said unto them, Be fruitful, and multiply, and replenish the earth, and subdue it: and have dominion over the fish of the sea, and over the fowl of the air, and over every living thing that moveth upon the earth.

Overview

This lesson is an overview of stewarding life—that is, of managing and balancing God's gifts to enable us to invest our lives in that which has lasting significance. Throughout the following twelve weeks, we will look at individual stewardship of specific gifts. For today, we will focus on understanding God's purposes and priorities for our lives.

Introduction

_____

_____

_____

I. The _____ of Life

A. Our _____ God

PSALM 36:9

9   For with thee is the fountain of life: in thy light shall we see light.

JEREMIAH 17:13

13   O LORD, the hope of Israel, all that forsake thee shall be ashamed, and they that depart from me shall be written in the earth, because they have forsaken the LORD, the fountain of living waters.

EXODUS 3:14

14   And God said unto Moses, I AM THAT I AM: and he said, Thus shalt thou say unto the children of Israel, I AM hath sent me unto you.

B. Our _____ God

GENESIS 1:26–28

26   And God said, Let us make man in our image, after our likeness: and let them have dominion over the fish of the sea, and over the fowl of the air, and over the cattle, and over all the earth, and over every creeping thing that creepeth upon the earth.

27   So God created man in his own image, in the image of God created he him; male and female created he them.

28 And God blessed them, and God said unto them, Be fruitful, and multiply, and replenish the earth, and subdue it: and have dominion over the fish of the sea, and over the fowl of the air, and over every living thing that moveth upon the earth.

EPHESIANS 4:24
24 And that ye put on the new man, which after God is created in righteousness and true holiness.

GENESIS 2:7
7 And the LORD God formed man of the dust of the ground, and breathed into his nostrils the breath of life; and man became a living soul.

II. The _____ of Life

A. *Because it is* _____ *by God*

JEREMIAH 1:5
5 Before I formed thee in the belly I knew thee; and before thou camest forth out of the womb I sanctified thee, and I ordained thee a prophet unto the nations.

LUKE 1:15
15 ...and he shall be filled with the Holy Ghost, even from his mother's womb.

PSALM 139:13–16
13 For thou hast possessed my reins: thou hast covered me in my mother's womb.
14 I will praise thee; for I am fearfully and wonderfully made: marvellous are thy works; and that my soul knoweth right well.

15 *My substance was not hid from thee, when I was made in secret, and curiously wrought in the lowest parts of the earth.*

16 *Thine eyes did see my substance, yet being unperfect; and in thy book all my members were written, which in continuance were fashioned, when as yet there was none of them.*

B. Because it is _____ by God

EXODUS 20:13

13 *Thou shalt not kill.*

GENESIS 9:6

6 *Whoso sheddeth man's blood, by man shall his blood be shed: for in the image of God made he man.*

ROMANS 13:4

4 *For he is the minister of God to thee for good. But if thou do that which is evil, be afraid; for he beareth not the sword in vain: for he is the minister of God, a revenger to execute wrath upon him that doeth evil.*

III. The _____ of _____ over Life

A. In the _____ of life

1. Sarah

GENESIS 18:13–14

13 *And the LORD said unto Abraham, Wherefore did Sarah laugh, saying, Shall I of a surety bear a child, which am old?*

14 Is any thing too hard for the LORD? At the time appointed I will return unto thee, according to the time of life, and Sarah shall have a son.

2. Hannah

1 SAMUEL 1:5, 19–20

5 But unto Hannah he gave a worthy portion; for he loved Hannah: but the LORD had shut up her womb.

19 And they rose up in the morning early, and worshipped before the LORD, and returned, and came to their house to Ramah: and Elkanah knew Hannah his wife; and the LORD remembered her.

20 Wherefore it came to pass, when the time was come about after Hannah had conceived, that she bare a son, and called his name Samuel, saying, Because I have asked him of the LORD.

3. Elisabeth

LUKE 1:7, 11–14

7 And they had no child, because that Elisabeth was barren, and they both were now well stricken in years.

11 And there appeared unto him an angel of the Lord standing on the right side of the altar of incense.

12 And when Zacharias saw him, he was troubled, and fear fell upon him.

13 But the angel said unto him, Fear not, Zacharias: for thy prayer is heard; and thy wife Elisabeth shall bear thee a son, and thou shalt call his name John.

14 And thou shalt have joy and gladness; and many shall rejoice at his birth.

B. In the _____ of life

DEUTERONOMY 30:15

15   See, I have set before thee this day life and good, and death and evil;

REVELATION 4:11

11   Thou art worthy, O LORD, to receive glory and honour and power: for thou hast created all things, and for thy pleasure they are and were created.

NUMBERS 14:21

21   But as truly as I live, all the earth shall be filled with the glory of the Lord.

MARK 16:15

15   And he said unto them, Go ye into all the world, and preach the gospel to every creature.

C. In the _____ of earthly life

GENESIS 6:17

17   And, behold, I, even I, do bring a flood of waters upon the earth, to destroy all flesh, wherein is the breath of life, from under heaven; and every thing that is in the earth shall die.

ROMANS 6:23

23   For the wages of sin is death; but the gift of God is eternal life through Jesus Christ our Lord.

ROMANS 5:12

12   Wherefore, as by one man sin entered into the world, and death by sin; and so death passed upon all men, for that all have sinned.

1 Samuel 2:6

6   *The Lord killeth, and maketh alive: he bringeth down to the grave, and bringeth up.*

Job 34:14–15

14   *If he set his heart upon man, if he gather unto himself his spirit and his breath;*

15   *All flesh shall perish together, and man shall turn again unto dust.*

Psalm 104:29

29   *Thou hidest thy face, they are troubled: thou takest away their breath, they die, and return to their dust.*

Isaiah 38:5

5   *Go, and say to Hezekiah, Thus saith the Lord, the God of David thy father, I have heard thy prayer, I have seen thy tears: behold, I will add unto thy days fifteen years.*

Psalm 73:17, 26

17   *Until I went into the sanctuary of God; then understood I their end.*

26   *My flesh and my heart faileth: but God is the strength of my heart, and my portion for ever.*

1 Kings 3:7

7   *And now, O Lord my God, thou hast made thy servant king instead of David my father: and I am but a little child: I know not how to go out or come in.*

IV. The _____ of Eternal Life

A. *From our* _____

ROMANS 6:23
23 For the wages of sin is **death**; but the gift of God is eternal life through Jesus Christ our Lord.

ROMANS 5:8
8 But God commendeth his love toward us, in that, while we were yet sinners, Christ **died** for us.

PSALM 49:15
15 But God will redeem my soul from the power of the grave: for he shall receive me. Selah.

1 JOHN 2:25
25 And this is the promise that he hath promised us, even eternal life.

B. *Because of the* _____

JOHN 11:25–27
25 Jesus said unto her, I am the resurrection, and the life: he that believeth in me, though he were dead, yet shall he live:
26 And whosoever liveth and believeth in me shall never die. Believest thou this?
27 She saith unto him, Yea, Lord: I believe that thou art the Christ, the Son of God, which should come into the world.

JOHN 14:6
6 Jesus saith unto him, I am the way, the truth, and the life: no man cometh unto the Father but by me.

Conclusion

JEREMIAH 1:5

5   *Before I formed thee in the belly I knew thee; and before thou camest forth out of the womb I sanctified thee, and I ordained thee a prophet unto the nations.*

MATTHEW 25:21

21   *His lord said unto him, Well done, thou good and faithful servant: thou hast been faithful over a few things, I will make thee ruler over many things: enter thou into the joy of thy lord.*

_____

_____

_____

Study Questions

1. What are the three basic methods by which people choose to appropriate the resources God has given to them?

2. What is our purpose on earth?

3. What truths do Jeremiah 1:5, Psalm 139:13–16, and Luke 1:15 teach?

4. In what three aspects of life did we study God's sovereignty?

5. Looking at the specific responsibilities God has given you, rate each one as to whether you have been squandering, spending, or stewarding that area of your life.

6. How have you seen God's purposes for creating you fulfilled in your life thus far?

7. One major aspect of living for God's glory is to make spreading the gospel a central part of our lives. Are you regularly sharing the gospel with lost people?

8. Throughout this lesson we have been speaking of the stewarding of our earthly lives. What about your eternal life? Write out your salvation testimony.

Memory Verse

1 KINGS 3:7

7   ...I am but a little child: I know not how to go out or come in.

Stewarding Time

Text

EPHESIANS 5:14–17

14 Wherefore he saith, Awake thou that sleepest, and arise from the dead, and Christ shall give thee light.

15 See then that ye walk circumspectly, not as fools, but as wise,

16 Redeeming the time, because the days are evil.

17 Wherefore be ye not unwise, but understanding what the will of the Lord is.

Overview

One of the greatest and most valuable gifts God has given to us is time. We are each given the same limited amount of time each day, and God teaches us His priorities for the stewardship of our time.

Introduction

_____

_____

_____

I. The _____ of Time

A. Awake to _____

EPHESIANS 5:14

14 *Wherefore he saith, Awake thou that sleepest, and arise from the dead, and Christ shall give thee light.*

ISAIAH 55:6–7

6 *Seek ye the LORD while he may be found, Call ye upon him while he is near:*

7 *Let the wicked forsake his way, and the unrighteous man his thoughts: and let him return unto the LORD, and he will have mercy upon him; and to our God, for he will abundantly pardon.*

ISAIAH 60:1

1 *Arise, shine; for thy light is come, and the glory of the LORD is risen upon thee.*

B. Awake to God's _____

II. The _____ of Time

A. A _____ walk

EPHESIANS 5:15

15 *See then that ye walk circumspectly, not as fools, but as wise,*

1 PETER 5:8

8   *Be sober, be vigilant; because your adversary the devil, as a roaring lion, walketh about, seeking whom he may devour.*

B. A _____ walk

EPHESIANS 5:16

16   *Redeeming the time, because the days are evil.*

MARK 13:33

33   *Take heed, watch and pray: for ye know not when the time is.*

EPHESIANS 5:15–16

15   *See then that ye walk circumspectly, not as fools, but as wise,*

16   *Redeeming the time, because the days are evil.*

III.   The _____ of Time

EPHESIANS 5:17

17   *Wherefore be ye not unwise, but understanding what the will of the Lord is.*

A. Seek the _____ of God

1.   Seek it in God's Word

PROVERBS 2:2–6

2   *So that thou incline thine ear unto wisdom, and apply thine heart to understanding;*

3   *Yea, if thou criest after knowledge, and liftest up thy voice for understanding;*

4   *If thou seekest her as silver, and searchest for her as for hid treasures;*
5   *Then shalt thou understand the fear of the* LORD, *and find the knowledge of God.*
6   *For the* LORD *giveth wisdom: out of his mouth cometh knowledge and understanding.*

2. Ask God for it

JAMES 1:5

5   *If any of you lack wisdom, let him ask of God, that giveth to all men liberally, and upbraideth not; and it shall be given him.*

3. Listen to the counsel of others

PROVERBS 1:5

5   *A wise man will hear, and will increase learning; and a man of understanding shall attain unto wise counsels:*

4. Through trial and error, apply it to our lives

PROVERBS 6:23

23   *For the commandment is a lamp; and the law is light; and reproofs of instruction are the way of life:*

PSALM 90:12

12   *So teach us to number our days, that we may apply our hearts unto wisdom.*

PSALM 39:4–5

4   LORD, *make me to know mine end, and the measure of my days, what it is; that I may know how frail I am.*

5   Behold, thou hast made my days as an handbreadth; and mine age is as nothing before thee: verily every man at his best state is altogether vanity. Selah.

B. Seek the _____ of God

JAMES 4:13
13   Go to now, ye that say, To day or to morrow we will go into such a city, and continue there a year, and buy and sell, and get gain.

JAMES 4:14
14   Whereas ye know not what shall be on the morrow. For what is your life? It is even a vapour, that appeareth for a little time, and then vanisheth away.

JAMES 4:15
15   For that ye ought to say, If the Lord will, we shall live, and do this, or that.

Conclusion

_____

_____

_____

Study Questions

1.   What three options do we have for the use of our time?

2.   In order, what are the two greatest gifts we have been given?

3.   Why do we need to be circumspect, or cautious and vigilant in our walk?

4.   What are the four ways we grow in wisdom?

5.   Describe when you "awoke" to salvation.

6. In what ways do you see your adversary the devil devour your time during your days and weeks?

7. Success is knowing and doing the will of God. On a scale of one to ten, where would you place your level of success?

8. What specific changes will you make in your schedule (or lack of schedule) this week to enable you to steward your time according to the will of God?

Memory Verse
PSALM 90:12
12 So teach us to number our days, that we may apply our hearts unto wisdom.

Stewarding Health

Text

1 CORINTHIANS 6:19–20

19 What? know ye not that your body is the temple of the Holy Ghost which is in you, which ye have of God, and ye are not your own?

20 For ye are bought with a price: therefore glorify God in your body, and in your spirit, which are God's.

Overview

Stewarding health is foundational to the Christian's ability to steward every other part of life. Our physical and emotional strength are vehicles through which we can minister to others for the Lord. The Bible outlines practical helps for caring for our physical and emotional wellbeing.

Introduction

_____

_____

_____

I. The _____ Paradigm for
  _____

3 John 2
2   *Beloved, I wish above all things that thou mayest prosper and be in health, even as thy soul prospereth.*

1 Corinthians 6:19–20
19   *What? know ye not that your body is the temple of the Holy Ghost which is in you, which ye have of God, and ye are not your own?*
20   *For ye are bought with a price: therefore glorify God in your body, and in your spirit, which are God's.*

Romans 8:28
28   *And we know that all things work together for good to them that love God, to them who are the called according to his purpose.*

Isaiah 38:1
1   *In those days was Hezekiah sick unto death…*

Isaiah 38:21
21   *Let them take a lump of figs, and lay it for a plaister upon the boil, and he shall recover.*

JOHN 9:2

2   And his disciples asked him, saying, Master, who did sin, this man, or his parents, that he was born blind?

JOHN 9:3

3   Neither hath this man sinned, nor his parents: but that the works of God should be made manifest in him.

II. The _____ of _____

A.   Eat for _____

DANIEL 1:5

5   And the king appointed them a daily provision of the king's meat, and of the wine which he drank: so nourishing them three years, that at the end thereof they might stand before the king.

DANIEL 1:8

8   But Daniel purposed in his heart that he would not defile himself with the portion of the king's meat, nor with the wine which he drank...

DANIEL 1:8, 12

8   ...therefore he requested of the prince of the eunuchs that he might not defile himself.
12   Prove thy servants, I beseech thee, ten days; and let them give us pulse to eat, and water to drink.

LEVITICUS 3:17

17   It shall be a perpetual statute for your generations throughout all your dwellings, that ye eat neither fat nor blood.

B. *Intensely* _____ *for* _____

- Moses—Exodus 34:28
- Elijah—1 Kings 19:8
- David—2 Samuel 12:16–23
- Jehoshaphat—2 Chronicles 20:3
- Josiah—Jeremiah 36:9
- Ezra—Ezra 10:6
- Nehemiah—Nehemiah 1:4
- Daniel—Daniel 10:3
- Esther—Esther 4:16
- Anna—Luke 2:37
- Jesus—Luke 4:1–2
- Paul—2 Corinthians 11:27
- Cornelius—Acts 10:30
- Church leaders and elders—Acts 14:23

III. The _____ from _____

1 KINGS 19:1–4

1 *And Ahab told Jezebel all that Elijah had done, and withal how he had slain all the prophets with the sword.*

2 *Then Jezebel sent a messenger unto Elijah, saying, So let the gods do to me, and more also, if I make not thy life as the life of one of them by to morrow about this time.*

3 *And when he saw that, he arose, and went for his life, and came to Beersheba, which belongeth to Judah, and left his servant there.*

4 *But he himself went a day's journey into the wilderness, and came and sat down under a juniper tree: and he requested for himself that he might die; and said, It is enough; now, O LORD, take away my life; for I am not better than my fathers.*

A. Find _____

1 KINGS 19:4

4   "But he himself went a day's journey into the wilderness…"

B. Take time to _____

1 KINGS 19:5, 6

5   …And as he lay and slept under a juniper tree…
6   …and laid him down again.

C. Receive _____

1 KINGS 19:5–6

5   …behold, then an angel touched him, and said unto him, Arise and eat.
6   And he looked, and, behold, there was a cake baken on the coals, and a cruse of water at his head. And he did eat and drink, and laid him down again.

Conclusion

ROMANS 15:4

4   For whatsoever things were written aforetime were written for our learning, that we through patience and comfort of the scriptures might have hope.

_____

_____

_____

Study Questions

1. What are the two kinds of health John referred to in 3 John 2?

2. What does 1 Corinthians 6:19–20 describe as the purpose for our bodies and spirits?

3. What incident of Jesus healing a man reminds us that even in days of illness or disease, God has a purpose bigger than we can immediately see?

4. What lessons do we learn from Elijah when Jezebel sought his life?

5. While much of our culture's emphasis on health panders to self-gratification, what should be our primary motivation for stewarding our health?

6. Compare your physical health to your spiritual health. Rate each on a scale of 1 to 10. What specific steps will you take to improve each of them?

7. Describe a sickness you or a loved one has experienced with no apparent cause. Purpose to believe God has a cause bigger than you can see.

8. The definition of a scriptural fast is "to restrict food for a spiritual purpose." Do you have any spiritual needs in your life for which you believe you should fast?

Memory Verse

1 CORINTHIANS 10:31
31 Whether therefore ye eat, or drink, or whatsoever ye do, do all to the glory of God.

Stewarding Energy

Text

MATTHEW 11:28–30

28 Come unto me, all ye that labour and are heavy laden, and I will give you rest.

29 Take my yoke upon you, and learn of me; for I am meek and lowly in heart: and ye shall find rest unto your souls.

30 For my yoke is easy, and my burden is light.

Overview

God equips us with everything we need to do His will. It is when we try to do His work (or our own) without seeking His priorities and utilizing His gift of rest that we begin to operate on overload. This lesson will examine God's way of redistributing these weights and relieving tension.

Introduction

_____

_____

_____

I. Plan for _____

- Activity overload
- Change overload
- Choice overload
- Commitment overload
- Debt overload
- Decision overload
- Expectation overload
- Fatigue overload
- Hurry overload
- Information overload
- Media overload
- Noise overload
- People overload
- Possession overload
- Technology overload
- Traffic overload
- Work overload

1 CORINTHIANS 10:13

13 There hath no temptation taken you but such as is common to man: but God is faithful, who will not suffer you to be tempted above that ye are able; but will with the temptation also make a way to escape, that ye may be able to bear it.

A. Schedule _____ *with God*

MARK 1:35

35 And in the morning, rising up a great while before day, he went out, and departed into a solitary place, and there prayed.

JOHN 4:34

34 Jesus saith unto them, My meat is to do the will of him that sent me, and to finish his work.

JOHN 6:38

38 For I came down from heaven, not to do mine own will, but the will of him that sent me.

B. Schedule time for God-given _____

- **Walk with God.**

  GENESIS 5:24

  24 And Enoch walked with God...

- **Care for your family.**

- **Labor at work.**

  EPHESIANS 6:5–7

  5 Servants, be obedient to them that are your masters according to the flesh, with fear and trembling, in singleness of your heart, as unto Christ;

  6 Not with eyeservice, as menpleasers; but as the servants of Christ, doing the will of God from the heart;

  7 With good will doing service, as to the Lord, and not to men.

- **Worship and serve God.**

HEBREWS 10:24–25

24 *And let us consider one another to provoke unto love and to good works:*

25 *Not forsaking the assembling of ourselves together, as the manner of some is; but exhorting one another: and so much the more, as ye see the day approaching.*

II. _____ for Replenishment

A. _____ *rest*

EXODUS 20:8–11

8 *Remember the sabbath day, to keep it holy.*

9 *Six days shalt thou labour, and do all thy work:*

10 *But the seventh day is the sabbath of the LORD thy God: in it thou shalt not do any work, thou, nor thy son, nor thy daughter, thy manservant, nor thy maidservant, nor thy cattle, nor thy stranger that is within thy gates:*

11 *For in six days the LORD made heaven and earth, the sea, and all that in them is, and rested the seventh day: wherefore the LORD blessed the sabbath day, and hallowed it.*

MARK 2:27

27 *And he said unto them, The sabbath was made for man, and not man for the sabbath:*

MARK 6:31–32

31 *And he said unto them, Come ye yourselves apart into a desert place, and rest a while: for there were many coming and going, and they had no leisure so much as to eat.*

32   *And they departed into a desert place by ship privately.*

MARK 6:46
46   *And when he had sent them away, he departed into a mountain to pray.*

PSALM 127:1–2
1   *Except the LORD build the house, they labour in vain that build it: except the LORD keep the city, the watchman waketh but in vain.*
2   *It is vain for you to rise up early, to sit up late, to eat the bread of sorrows: for so he giveth his beloved sleep.*

B. _____ *rest*

MATTHEW 11:28–30
28   *Come unto me, all ye that labour and are heavy laden, and I will give you rest.*
29   *Take my yoke upon you, and learn of me; for I am meek and lowly in heart: and ye shall find rest unto your souls.*
30   *For my yoke is easy, and my burden is light.*

Conclusion

_____

_____

_____

Study Questions

1. How did Jesus replenish Himself so He could freely give to the needs of others?

2. According to John 6:38, what was the center of Jesus' life?

3. How does Genesis 5:24 sum up Enoch's life?

4. What kind of rest does Christ speak of in Matthew 11:28–30?

5. What are some biblical priorities we should say "yes" to?

6. What areas in your life need more margin? What are some steps you can take toward adding margin to your life?

7. What are some God-given priorities you have been neglecting? What incidentals can you say "no" to?

8. What kind of physical burdens in our lives can truly affect our health? To what extent do you see these in your own life, and what will you do in response to recognizing them?

Memory Verse

JOHN 6:38
38 For I came down from heaven, not to do mine own will, but the will of him that sent me.

Stewarding Thoughts
(Part One)

Text

PHILIPPIANS 4:4–8

4   Rejoice in the Lord alway: and again I say, Rejoice.

5   Let your moderation be known unto all men. The Lord is at hand.

6   Be careful for nothing; but in every thing by prayer and supplication with thanksgiving let your requests be made known unto God.

7   And the peace of God, which passeth all understanding, shall keep your hearts and minds through Christ Jesus.

8   Finally, brethren, whatsoever things are true, whatsoever things are honest, whatsoever things are just, whatsoever things are pure, whatsoever things are lovely, whatsoever things are of good report; if there be any virtue, and if there be any praise, think on these things.

Overview

Our thoughts control our perception of not only life, but of who God is in relation to our lives. In this lesson and our next lesson, we will study the necessity, as well as God's method, for stewarding our thoughts.

Introduction

_____

_____

_____

ROMANS 12:2

2   ...be ye transformed by the renewing of your mind.

PHILIPPIANS 4:4–8

4   Rejoice in the Lord alway: and again I say, Rejoice.

5   Let your moderation be known unto all men. The Lord is at hand.

6   Be careful for nothing; but in every thing by prayer and supplication with thanksgiving let your requests be made known unto God.

7   And the peace of God, which passeth all understanding, shall keep your hearts and minds through Christ Jesus.

8   Finally, brethren, whatsoever things are true, whatsoever things are honest, whatsoever things are just, whatsoever things are pure, whatsoever things are lovely, whatsoever things are of good report; if there be any virtue, and if there be any praise, think on these things.

I.   Think with _____

PHILIPPIANS 4:4

4   Rejoice in the Lord alway: and again I say, Rejoice.

A. The _____ of praise

DEUTERONOMY 10:21

21   He is thy praise, and he is thy God, that hath done for thee these great and terrible things, which thine eyes have seen.

B. The _____ *of praise*

ACTS 5:41

41 *And they departed from the presence of the council, rejoicing that they were counted worthy to suffer shame for his name.*

PSALM 28:7

7 *The LORD is my strength and my shield; my heart trusted in him, and I am helped: therefore my heart greatly rejoiceth; and with my song will I praise him.*

II. Think with _____

REVELATION 12:10

10 *And I heard a loud voice saying in heaven, Now is come salvation, and strength, and the kingdom of our God, and the power of his Christ: for the **accuser of our brethren** is cast down, which accused them before our God day and night.*

PHILIPPIANS 4:5

5 *Let your moderation be known unto all men. The Lord is at hand.*

A. Rest in His _____

PSALM 46:10

10 *Be still, and know that I am God...*

PSALM 56:9

9 *When I cry unto thee, then shall mine enemies turn back: this I know; for God is for me.*

Hebrews 13:5–6

5   *Let your conversation be without covetousness; and be content with such things as ye have: for he hath said, I will never leave thee, nor forsake thee.*

6   *So that we may boldly say, The Lord is my helper, and I will not fear what man shall do unto me.*

B. Rest in His _____

Job 23:10

10   *But he knoweth the way that I take: when he hath tried me, I shall come forth as gold.*

Conclusion

_____

_____

_____

Study Questions

1. According to Romans 12:2, what is the key to confronting stress and anxious thinking?

2. What are some ways our minds can be wasted by *overuse*?

3. What/Who does Philippians 4:4 say should be the object of our praise?

4. In what attribute of God did Job find peace?

5. Philippians 4:4 admonishes us to rejoice in the Lord always. What circumstance in the past week has kept your heart from rejoicing?

6. What are some reasons for praising Jesus Christ? Whenever you feel stress and anxiety coming on during the week, purpose to think on the reasons you can praise our perfect and unchanging object of praise.

7. What are some of the opponents of praise in your life?

8. How can you combat the lies of Satan in your life this week?

Memory Verse

ROMANS 12:2
2 *And be not conformed to this world: but be ye transformed by the renewing of your mind, that ye may prove what is that good, and acceptable, and perfect, will of God.*

Stewarding Thoughts
(Part Two)

Text

PHILIPPIANS 4:4–8

4 Rejoice in the Lord alway: and again I say, Rejoice.

5 Let your moderation be known unto all men. The Lord is at hand.

6 Be careful for nothing; but in every thing by prayer and supplication with thanksgiving let your requests be made known unto God.

7 And the peace of God, which passeth all understanding, shall keep your hearts and minds through Christ Jesus.

8 Finally, brethren, whatsoever things are true, whatsoever things are honest, whatsoever things are just, whatsoever things are pure, whatsoever things are lovely, whatsoever things are of good report; if there be any virtue, and if there be any praise, think on these things.

Overview

In our stressed-out society, where our minds are flooded with anxiety and care, God's Word has the prescription for peace for the Christian. In this lesson we are continuing our study of stewarding our thoughts, using the directives from Philippians 4.

Introduction

_____
_____
_____

I.   Think with _____

PHILIPPIANS 4:6
6   Be careful for nothing; but in every thing by prayer and supplication with thanksgiving let your requests be made known unto God.

A. *Request without* _____

PSALM 56:3
3   What time I am afraid, I will trust in thee.

B. *Request with* _____

HEBREWS 13:8
8   Jesus Christ the same yesterday, and to day, and for ever.

1 THESSALONIANS 5:18
18   In every thing give thanks: for this is the will of God in Christ Jesus concerning you.

II. Think with _____

A. _____ *design*

ROMANS 5:1
1   Therefore being justified by faith, we have peace with God through our Lord Jesus Christ.

ISAIAH 26:3

3   *Thou wilt keep him in perfect peace, whose mind is stayed on thee: because he trusteth in thee.*

B. _____ *design*

PHILIPPIANS 4:7

7   *...the peace of God, which passeth all understanding, shall keep your hearts and minds...*

COLOSSIANS 3:15

15   *And let the peace of God rule in your hearts...*

III. Think with _____

A. The _____ *of pure thoughts*

PHILIPPIANS 4:8

8   *Finally, brethren, whatsoever things are true, whatsoever things are honest, whatsoever things are just, whatsoever things are pure, whatsoever things are lovely, whatsoever things are of good report; if there be any virtue, and if there be any praise, think on these things.*

B. The _____ *of pure thoughts*

2 CORINTHIANS 10:5

5   *Casting down imaginations, and every high thing that exalteth itself against the knowledge of God, and bringing into captivity every thought to the obedience of Christ.*

Conclusion

Lord,

*Today, I want to **praise** You because Your sacrifice for me is immeasurable, and Your love for me is unfathomable. I praise You because You are merciful and faithful to me.*

*Today, I want to express **poise**, real moderation and peaceableness because You are sovereign and You are at hand. With poise, I want to model joy in ministry and family life. Help me not to worry, but to live peaceably. Remind me to place rest and margin on my schedule that I may hear Your voice.*

*Today, I want to **pray** with supplication for Your power and filling. I surrender myself, my tendencies, my past, present, and future to You because of the cross. I ask You to help me make this world less to me, and for Your power to dominate my heart. I thank You for saving me and providing for me. I thank You for a loving family and the privilege to serve You.*

*Today, I pray for the **peace** that passes all understanding. Give me peace that comes from a proper vision of You and faith in Your sovereignty. Help me to sleep well.*

*Today, I want to practice **pure** thinking, positively meditating on that which is lovely, pure, and true. I ask You to renew my mind today through Your Word.*

_____

_____

_____

Study Questions

1. Through what avenue does God ask us to bring our burdens and stresses to Him?

2. What are the two kinds of peace God offers us?

3. How do we fix our minds on Christ?

4. How can we develop pure thinking patterns?

5. According to Psalm 56:3, we should turn our fears over to the Lord and trust God in spite of them. What are some fears you have been holding on to?

6. God offers you peace in exchange for your anxiety. What are some areas in your life that you have allowed to become infested with worry and anxiety?

7. Are there any negative influences in your life that are corrupting your biblical thinking? If so, what steps will you take to purge them out of your life?

8. To steward our thoughts honestly, we need to move beyond simply knowing truths, to applying and living them. What are some practical ways you are going to apply these truths on stewarding your thoughts this week?

Memory Verse

2 CORINTHIANS 10:5

5 Casting down imaginations, and every high thing that exalteth itself against the knowledge of God, and bringing into captivity every thought to the obedience of Christ.

Stewarding Trials

Text

2 CORINTHIANS 12:1–10

1   It is not expedient for me doubtless to glory. I will come to visions and revelations of the Lord.

2   I knew a man in Christ above fourteen years ago, (whether in the body, I cannot tell; or whether out of the body, I cannot tell: God knoweth;) such an one caught up to the third heaven.

3   And I knew such a man, (whether in the body, or out of the body, I cannot tell: God knoweth;)

4   How that he was caught up into paradise, and heard unspeakable words, which it is not lawful for a man to utter.

5   Of such an one will I glory: yet of myself I will not glory, but in mine infirmities.

6   For though I would desire to glory, I shall not be a fool; for I will say the truth: but now I forbear, lest any man should think of me above that which he seeth me to be, or that he heareth of me.

7   And lest I should be exalted above measure through the abundance of the revelations, there was given to me a thorn in the flesh, the messenger of Satan to buffet me, lest I should be exalted above measure.

8   For this thing I besought the Lord thrice, that it might depart from me.

9   And he said unto me, My grace is sufficient for thee: for my strength is made perfect in weakness. Most gladly therefore will I rather glory in my infirmities, that the power of Christ may rest upon me.

10   Therefore I take pleasure in infirmities, in reproaches, in necessities, in persecutions, in distresses for Christ's sake: for when I am weak, then am I strong.

Overview

We don't often think of trials as gifts to steward, but rather as circumstances to avoid. Through the testimonies of Paul and Job, we will examine God's wonderful workings in lives that have purposed to steward trials for God, through His strength.

Introduction

_____

_____

_____

Job 2:9
9 Dost thou still retain thine integrity? curse God, and die.

Job 2:10
10 Thou speakest as one of the foolish women speaketh. What? shall we receive good at the hand of God, and shall we not receive evil?

Job 30:26
26 When I looked for good, then evil came unto me: and when I waited for light, there came darkness.

I. _____

2 Corinthians 12:2–4
2 I knew a man in Christ above fourteen years ago, (whether in the body, I cannot tell; or whether out of the body, I cannot tell: God knoweth;) such an one caught up to the third heaven.
3 And I knew such a man, (whether in the body, or out of the body, I cannot tell: God knoweth;)
4 How that he was caught up into paradise, and heard unspeakable words, which it is not lawful for a man to utter.

A. The _____ of the trial
Galatians 4:13, 15
13 Ye know how through infirmity of the flesh I preached the gospel unto you at the first.

15 Where is then the blessedness ye spake of? for I bear you record, that, if it had been possible, ye would have plucked out your own eyes, and have given them to me.

2 CORINTHIANS 12:8
8 For this thing I besought the Lord thrice, that it might depart from me.

B. The _____ of the trial

2 PETER 1:21
21 For the prophecy came not in old time by the will of man: but holy men of God spake as they were moved by the Holy Ghost.

2 CORINTHIANS 11:24–28
24 Of the Jews five times received I forty stripes save one.
25 Thrice was I beaten with rods, once was I stoned, thrice I suffered shipwreck, a night and a day I have been in the deep;
26 In journeyings often, in perils of waters, in perils of robbers, in perils by mine own countrymen, in perils by the heathen, in perils in the city, in perils in the wilderness, in perils in the sea, in perils among false brethren;
27 In weariness and painfulness, in watchings often, in hunger and thirst, in fastings often, in cold and nakedness.
28 Beside those things that are without, that which cometh upon me daily, the care of all the churches.

2 CORINTHIANS 12:7–10
7 And lest I should be exalted above measure through the abundance of the revelations, there was given to me a thorn in the flesh, the messenger of Satan to buffet me, lest I should be exalted above measure.

8   For this thing I besought the Lord thrice, that it might depart from me.

9   And he said unto me, My grace is sufficient for thee: for my strength is made perfect in weakness. Most gladly therefore will I rather glory in my infirmities, that the power of Christ may rest upon me.

10   Therefore I take pleasure in infirmities, in reproaches, in necessities, in persecutions, in distresses for Christ's sake: for when I am weak, then am I strong.

C. The _____ of the trial

MARK 14:65

65   And some began to spit on him, and to cover his face, and to buffet him, and to say unto him, Prophesy: and the servants did strike him with the palms of their hands.

JOB 1:9–11

9   Then Satan answered the LORD, and said, Doth Job fear God for nought?

10   Hast not thou made an hedge about him, and about his house, and about all that he hath on every side? thou hast blessed the work of his hands, and his substance is increased in the land.

11   But put forth thine hand now, and touch all that he hath, and he will curse thee to thy face.

ROMANS 8:28

28   And we know that all things work together for good to them that love God, to them who are the called according to his purpose.

II. _____

2 CORINTHIANS 12:9–10

9   And he said unto me, My grace is sufficient for thee: for my strength is made perfect in weakness. Most gladly therefore will I rather glory in my infirmities, that the power of Christ may rest upon me.

10   Therefore I take pleasure in infirmities, in reproaches, in necessities, in persecutions, in distresses for Christ's sake: for when I am weak, then am I strong.

A. _____ *by the grace of God*

B. _____ *by the grace of God*

JOB 23:10

10   But he knoweth the way that I take: when he hath tried me, I shall come forth as gold.

1 PETER 1:7

7   That the trial of your faith, being much more precious than of gold that perisheth, though it be tried with fire, might be found unto praise and honour and glory at the appearing of Jesus Christ.

III. _____

A. *Through His* _____

1 CORINTHIANS 10:13

13   There hath no temptation taken you but such as is common to man: but God is faithful, who will not suffer

you to be tempted above that ye are able; but will with the temptation also make a way to escape, that ye may be able to bear it.

B. *Through His* _____

1. Trust God's ways

JAMES 1:3–4

3   Knowing this, that the trying of your faith worketh patience.

4   But let patience have her perfect work, that ye may be perfect and entire, wanting nothing.

PSALM 31:15

15   My times are in thy hand…

2. Seek God's wisdom

JAMES 1:5

5   If any of you lack wisdom, let him ask of God, that giveth to all men liberally, and upbraideth not; and it shall be given him.

3. Rest in God's love

ROMANS 5:3–5

3   And not only so, but we glory in tribulations also: knowing that tribulation worketh patience;

4   And patience, experience; and experience, hope:

5   And hope maketh not ashamed; because the love of God is shed abroad in our hearts by the Holy Ghost which is given unto us.

Conclusion

Study Questions

1. How did Job choose to steward the hardest trial of his life, as seen in his response to his wife?

2. What is meant by *stewarding* trials?

3. What was responsible for most of the effectiveness in Paul's life?

4. During which times does God's grace purify our lives and mature our faith?

5. Write about a trial you have gone through in which you have (either at the time or later) seen God's purpose.

6. Write about a time when you have especially seen God's grace sufficient for you—a time when you couldn't have made it without His grace.

7. As you reflect on your own life, have you allowed God to graciously humble you through your trials, or have you distrusted Him?

8. Share an experience from your life when you have only held the dark, heavy box of a trial and become angry at God. Also share an experience where you have opened the box and enjoyed the benefits and blessings God had for you through that trial.

Memory Verse

2 CORINTHIANS 12:10

10 Therefore I take pleasure in infirmities, in reproaches, in necessities, in persecutions, in distresses for Christ's sake: for when I am weak, then am I strong.

Stewarding Resources

Text

MATTHEW 25:14–30

14 For the kingdom of heaven is as a man travelling into a far country, who called his own servants, and delivered unto them his goods.

15 And unto one he gave five talents, to another two, and to another one; to every man according to his several ability; and straightway took his journey.

16 Then he that had received the five talents went and traded with the same, and made them other five talents.

17 And likewise he that had received two, he also gained other two.

18 But he that had received one went and digged in the earth, and hid his lord's money.

19 After a long time the lord of those servants cometh, and reckoneth with them.

20 And so he that had received five talents came and brought other five talents, saying, Lord, thou deliveredst unto me five talents: behold, I have gained beside them five talents more.

21 His lord said unto him, Well done, thou good and faithful servant: thou hast been faithful over a few things, I will make thee ruler over many things: enter thou into the joy of thy lord.

22 He also that had received two talents came and said, Lord, thou deliveredst unto me two talents: behold, I have gained two other talents beside them.

23 His lord said unto him, Well done, good and faithful servant; thou hast been faithful over a few things, I will make thee ruler over many things: enter thou into the joy of thy lord.

24 Then he which had received the one talent came and said, Lord, I knew thee that thou art an hard man, reaping where thou hast not sown, and gathering where thou hast not strawed:

25 And I was afraid, and went and hid thy talent in the earth: lo, there thou hast that is thine.

26 His lord answered and said unto him, Thou wicked and slothful servant, thou knewest that I reap where I sowed not, and gather where I have not strawed:

27 Thou oughtest therefore to have put my money to the exchangers, and then at my coming I should have received mine own with usury.

28 Take therefore the talent from him, and give it unto him which hath ten talents.

29 For unto every one that hath shall be given, and he shall have abundance: but from him that hath not shall be taken away even that which he hath.

30 And cast ye the unprofitable servant into outer darkness: there shall be weeping and gnashing of teeth.

Overview

While we have many gifts from God—health, time, relationships, etc.—our finances are one of the few *tangible* assets we are given to steward for His glory. Through Jesus' parable of the three stewards and the talents, in this lesson we will study finances from God's perspective.

Introduction

_____

_____

_____

MATTHEW 6:21
21   For where your treasure is, there will your heart be also.

I.   The Distribution of _____

MATTHEW 25:14–15
14   For the kingdom of heaven is as a man travelling into a far country, who called his own servants, and delivered unto them his goods.
15   And unto one he gave five talents, to another two, and to another one; to every man according to his several ability; and straightway took his journey.

A.   The _____ of _____

JAMES 1:17
17   Every good gift and every perfect gift is from above, and cometh down from the Father of lights, with whom is no variableness, neither shadow of turning.

PSALM 24:1
1   The earth is the LORD's, and the fulness thereof; the world, and they that dwell therein.

1 CHRONICLES 29:10–12
10   Wherefore David blessed the LORD before all the congregation: and David said, Blessed be thou, LORD God of Israel our father, for ever and ever.

11   Thine, O Lord is the greatness, and the power, and the glory, and the victory, and the majesty: for all that is in the heaven and in the earth is thine; thine is the kingdom, O Lord, and thou art exalted as head above all.

12   Both riches and honour come of thee, and thou reignest over all; and in thine hand is power and might; and in thine hand it is to make great, and to give strength unto all.

B. The _____ of His _____

1 Corinthians 4:2

2   Moreover it is required in stewards, that a man be found faithful.

II. The Demonstration of _____

A. The _____ stewards

Matthew 25:16–17

16   Then he that had received the five talents went and traded with the same, and made them other five talents.

17   And likewise he that had received two, he also gained other two.

1 Timothy 6:9

9   But they that will be rich fall into temptation and a snare, and into many foolish and hurtful lusts, which drown men in destruction and perdition.

B. The _____ steward

Matthew 25:18

18   But he that had received one went and digged in the earth, and hid his lord's money.

III. The Day of _____

A. A call to _____

MATTHEW 25:19

19 After a long time the lord of those servants cometh, and reckoneth with them.

B. A commendation to the _____

MATTHEW 25:20–23

20 And so he that had received five talents came and brought other five talents, saying, Lord, thou deliveredst unto me five talents: behold, I have gained beside them five talents more.

21 His lord said unto him, Well done, thou good and faithful servant: thou hast been faithful over a few things, I will make thee ruler over many things: enter thou into the joy of thy lord.

22 He also that had received two talents came and said, Lord, thou deliveredst unto me two talents: behold, I have gained two other talents beside them.

23 His lord said unto him, Well done, good and faithful servant; thou hast been faithful over a few things, I will make thee ruler over many things: enter thou into the joy of thy lord.

- **Work diligently**

  PROVERBS 10:4

  4   He becometh poor that dealeth with a slack hand: but the hand of the diligent maketh rich.

  PROVERBS 12:24

  24   The hand of the diligent shall bear rule: but the slothful shall be under tribute.

PROVERBS 13:4

4   *The soul of the sluggard desireth, and hath nothing: but the soul of the diligent shall be made fat.*

PROVERBS 21:5

5   *The thoughts of the diligent tend only to plenteousness; but of every one that is hasty only to want.*

PROVERBS 22:29

29   *Seest thou a man diligent in his business? he shall stand before kings; he shall not stand before mean men.*

- **Transfer ownership.**

- **Steward efficiently.**

  1 TIMOTHY 6:6–8

  6   *But godliness with contentment is great gain.*

  7   *For we brought nothing into this world, and it is certain we can carry nothing out.*

  8   *And having food and raiment let us be therewith content.*

- **Save regularly.**

  PROVERBS 11:16

  16   *A gracious woman retaineth honour: and strong men retain riches.*

- **Give generously.**

  2 CORINTHIANS 8:1–3

  1   *Moreover, brethren, we do you to wit of the grace of God bestowed on the churches of Macedonia;*

  2   *How that in a great trial of affliction the abundance of their joy and their deep poverty abounded unto the riches of their liberality.*

3 For to their power, I bear record, yea, and beyond their power they were willing of themselves.

2 CORINTHIANS 9:7

7 Every man according as he purposeth in his heart, so let him give; not grudgingly, or of necessity: for God loveth a cheerful giver.

C. A condemnation of the _____

_____

MATTHEW 25:24–25

24 Then he which had received the one talent came and said, Lord, I knew thee that thou art an hard man, reaping where thou hast not sown, and gathering where thou hast not strawed:

25 And I was afraid, and went and hid thy talent in the earth: lo, there thou hast that is thine.

MATTHEW 25:26–30

26 His lord answered and said unto him, Thou wicked and slothful servant, thou knewest that I reap where I sowed not, and gather where I have not strawed:

27 Thou oughtest therefore to have put my money to the exchangers, and then at my coming I should have received mine own with usury.

28 Take therefore the talent from him, and give it unto him which hath ten talents.

29 For unto every one that hath shall be given, and he shall have abundance: but from him that hath not shall be taken away even that which he hath.

30 And cast ye the unprofitable servant into outer darkness: there shall be weeping and gnashing of teeth.

1 TIMOTHY 6:17

17 *Charge them that are rich in this world, that they be not highminded, nor trust in uncertain riches, but in the living God, who giveth us richly all things to enjoy.*

Conclusion

ROMANS 14:10–12

10 *But why dost thou judge thy brother? or why dost thou set at nought thy brother? for we shall all stand before the judgment seat of Christ.*
11 *For it is written, As I live, saith the Lord, every knee shall bow to me, and every tongue shall confess to God.*
12 *So then every one of us shall give account of himself to God.*

LUKE 16:10–11

10 *He that is faithful in that which is least is faithful also in much: and he that is unjust in the least is unjust also in much.*
11 *If therefore ye have not been faithful in the unrighteous mammon, who will commit to your trust the true riches?*

MATTHEW 25:21

21 *Well done, thou good and faithful servant: thou hast been faithful over a few things, I will make thee ruler over many things: enter thou into the joy of thy lord.*

_____

_____

_____

Study Questions

1. In how many of Jesus' thirty-eight parables did He speak about money or possessions?

2. Who/What does our security come from?

3. What is the single determining characteristic of a steward's success?

4. What did the unfaithful servant's burying the money in the ground show about his motives?

5. There is great security in recognizing God as the owner of all things. To this point, have you looked for security in God or finances?

6. Some people eagerly promise that if they had great resources, they would gladly give all to the Lord's work, and to diligently live by a budget. How are you doing with stewarding the resources you *already* have?

7. Five easily distinguishable habits are consistently present in those who wisely handle finances: working diligently, transferring ownership, stewarding efficiently, saving regularly, and giving generously. In which of these areas are you strong, and on which ones do you need to work?

8. Financial stewardship is in many ways baseline to every other area of stewardship. Based on your stewarding of your finances, how would you say you are stewarding the other areas of your life?

Memory Verse

LUKE 16:10
10 *He that is faithful in that which is least is faithful also in much: and he that is unjust in the least is unjust also in much.*

Stewarding Friendship

Text

EPHESIANS 4:25–32

25 Wherefore putting away lying, speak every man truth with his neighbour: for we are members one of another.

26 Be ye angry, and sin not: let not the sun go down upon your wrath:

27 Neither give place to the devil.

28 Let him that stole steal no more: but rather let him labour, working with his hands the thing which is good, that he may have to give to him that needeth.

29 Let no corrupt communication proceed out of your mouth, but that which is good to the use of edifying, that it may minister grace unto the hearers.

30 And grieve not the holy Spirit of God, whereby ye are sealed unto the day of redemption.

31 Let all bitterness, and wrath, and anger, and clamour, and evil speaking, be put away from you, with all malice:

32 And be ye kind one to another, tenderhearted, forgiving one another, even as God for Christ's sake hath forgiven you.

Overview

God designed us with a need for friendships. True, godly friendship is founded on a mutual walk with the Lord and can bring us great fulfillment. Stewarding friendship includes both *having* friends and *being* a friend. In this lesson, we will learn through Ephesians 4 how to develop and steward friendships for the glory of God.

Introduction

_____

_____

_____

I. Steward with _____

A. *Vanquish* _____

EPHESIANS 4:25
*25   Wherefore putting away lying, speak every man truth
with his neighbour: for we are members one of another.*

PSALM 15:1–2
*1   LORD, who shall abide in thy tabernacle? who shall
dwell in thy holy hill?*
*2   He that walketh uprightly, and worketh righteousness,
and speaketh the truth in his heart.*

B. *Value* _____

EPHESIANS 4:15
*15   But speaking the truth in love, may grow up into him
in all things, which is the head, even Christ.*

PROVERBS 27:6
*6   Faithful are the wounds of a friend; but the kisses of
an enemy are deceitful.*

II. Steward with _____

PROVERBS 17:17
*17 A friend loveth at all times, and a brother is born
for adversity.*

A. Anger destroys _____

EPHESIANS 4:26
26 Be ye angry, and sin not: let not the sun go down upon your wrath:

EPHESIANS 4:31
31 Let all bitterness, and wrath, and anger, and clamour, and evil speaking, be put away from you, with all malice:

PROVERBS 22:24–25
24 Make no friendship with an angry man; and with a furious man thou shalt not go:
25 Lest thou learn his ways, and get a snare to thy soul.

JAMES 1:20
20 For the wrath of man worketh not the righteousness of God.

B. Anger invites Satanic _____

EPHESIANS 4:26–27
26 Be ye angry, and sin not: let not the sun go down upon your wrath:
27 Neither give place to the devil.

HEBREWS 12:15
15 Looking diligently lest any man fail of the grace of God; lest any root of bitterness springing up trouble you, and thereby many be defiled.

2 CORINTHIANS 2:10–11
10 To whom ye forgive any thing, I forgive also: for if I forgave any thing, to whom I forgave it, for your sakes forgave I it in the person of Christ;

11   *Lest Satan should get an advantage of us: for we are not ignorant of his devices.*

EPHESIANS 4:32
32   *And be ye kind one to another, tenderhearted, forgiving one another, even as God for Christ's sake hath forgiven you.*

III. Steward with _____

A. _____ *in our* _____

JAMES 4:4
4   *Ye adulterers and adulteresses, know ye not that the friendship of the world is enmity with God? whosoever therefore will be a friend of the world is the enemy of God.*

LUKE 19:10
10   *For the Son of man is come to seek and to save that which was lost.*

JAMES 2:23
23   *And the scripture was fulfilled which saith, Abraham believed God, and it was imputed unto him for righteousness: and he was called the Friend of God.*

B. _____ *in* _____

EPHESIANS 4:29
29   *Let no corrupt communication proceed out of your mouth, but that which is good to the use of edifying, that it may minister grace unto the hearers.*

COLOSSIANS 4:6
6   *Let your speech be alway with grace, seasoned with salt, that ye may know how ye ought to answer every man.*

PROVERBS 27:17

17 Iron sharpeneth iron; so a man sharpeneth the countenance of his friend.

PROVERBS 17:17

17 A friend loveth at all times, and a brother is born for adversity.

C. _____ *in* _____

MATTHEW 18:21–22

21 Then came Peter to him, and said, Lord, how oft shall my brother sin against me, and I forgive him? till seven times?
22 Jesus saith unto him, I say not unto thee, Until seven times: but, Until seventy times seven.

EPHESIANS 4:32

32 And be ye kind one to another, tenderhearted, forgiving one another, even as God for Christ's sake hath forgiven you.

Conclusion

EPHESIANS 4:25

25 Wherefore putting away lying, speak every man truth with his neighbour: for we are members one of another.

_____

_____

_____

Study Questions

1. What does God specifically command us to do to build lasting, edifying relationships?

2. According to Ephesians 4:15, what is truth's best friend?

3. According to Ephesians 4:31, what are the six subsets of anger?

4. As Christians, who should our closest friends be?

5. Truth in relationships is a reflection of a heart of integrity. Can your spouse and your friends trust you? Implicitly?

6. Are you reaping any consequences of your anger in your relationships? What steps will you take this week to repair the damage?

7. When we become bitter, we hurt ourselves more than anyone else. Can you pinpoint bitterness that you are carrying? How is bitterness affecting you? Your children?

8. Do you more often find yourself being a scorekeeper or a grace giver?

Memory Verse

EPHESIANS 4:29
29 Let no corrupt communication proceed out of your mouth, but that which is good to the use of edifying, that it may minister grace unto the hearers.

Stewarding Family

Text

Deuteronomy 6:4–9

4   Hear, O Israel: The Lord our God is one Lord:

5   And thou shalt love the Lord thy God with all thine heart, and with all thy soul, and with all thy might.

6   And these words, which I command thee this day, shall be in thine heart:

7   And thou shalt teach them diligently unto thy children, and shalt talk of them when thou sittest in thine house, and when thou walkest by the way, and when thou liest down, and when thou risest up.

8   And thou shalt bind them for a sign upon thine hand, and they shall be as frontlets between thine eyes.

9   And thou shalt write them upon the posts of thy house, and on thy gates.

Overview

No one has as much influence over children as their parents. In this lesson we will study the Scriptural mandates for bringing up our children and stewarding the precious gift of our family.

Introduction

_____

_____

_____

I. _____ **of the Scriptures**

DEUTERONOMY 6:4–9

4   *Hear, O Israel: The LORD our God is one LORD:*

5   *And thou shalt love the LORD thy God with all thine heart, and with all thy soul, and with all thy might.*

6   *And these words, which I command thee this day, shall be in thine heart:*

7   *And thou shalt teach them diligently unto thy children, and shalt talk of them when thou sittest in thine house, and when thou walkest by the way, and when thou liest down, and when thou risest up.*

8   *And thou shalt bind them for a sign upon thine hand, and they shall be as frontlets between thine eyes.*

9   *And thou shalt write them upon the posts of thy house, and on thy gates.*

A. _____ *to the parents*

B. _____ *to the children*

DEUTERONOMY 6:7

7   *And thou shalt teach them diligently unto thy children, and shalt talk of them when thou sittest in thine house, and when thou walkest by the way, and when thou liest down, and when thou risest up.*

II. _____ of the Parents

A. A testimony of _____

EPHESIANS 6:4

4   And, ye fathers, provoke not your children to wrath: but bring them up in the nurture and admonition of the Lord.

COLOSSIANS 3:21

21   Fathers, provoke not your children to anger, lest they be discouraged.

1 THESSALONIANS 2:11

11   As ye know how we exhorted and comforted and charged every one of you, as a father doth his children.

B. A testimony of _____

PROVERBS 29:17

17   Correct thy son, and he shall give thee rest; yea, he shall give delight unto thy soul.

III. _____ of Salvation

A. A _____ in Scripture

2 TIMOTHY 1:5–6

5   When I call to remembrance the unfeigned faith that is in thee, which dwelt first in thy grandmother Lois, and thy mother Eunice; and I am persuaded that in thee also.
6   Wherefore I put thee in remembrance that thou stir up the gift of God, which is in thee by the putting on of my hands.

2 Timothy 3:14–15

14 *But continue thou in the things which thou hast learned and hast been assured of, knowing of whom thou hast learned them;*

15 *And that from a child thou hast known the holy scriptures, which are able to make thee wise unto salvation through faith which is in Christ Jesus.*

B. A _____ *in Heaven*

Romans 10:17

17 *So then faith cometh by hearing, and hearing by the word of God.*

Conclusion

Galatians 6:9

9 *And let us not be weary in well doing: for in due season we shall reap, if we faint not.*

_____

_____

_____

Study Questions

1. According to Deuteronomy 6:4–9, what is the first step in teaching our children truths about God?

2. When and where should we strive to instill God's truths into our children?

3. How do you spell love?

4. What do your children need most from you?

5. What specifically will you do this week to increase the amount of time you spend with your children?

6. What can you add to your life and home to enable you to pass on truths to your children?

7. On a scale of 1–10, to what degree do you provoke your children to anger? What steps will you begin implementing this week to encourage, rather than discourage your children?

8. Do you have family devotions in your home? If not, commit to begin this week. If so, how can you improve the nurturing aspect of them?

Memory Verse

PSALM 127:3

3 Lo, children are an heritage of the LORD: and the fruit of the womb is his reward.

Stewarding Influence

Text

GENESIS 37:1–11

1   And Jacob dwelt in the land wherein his father was a stranger, in the land of Canaan.

2   These are the generations of Jacob. Joseph, being seventeen years old, was feeding the flock with his brethren; and the lad was with the sons of Bilhah, and with the sons of Zilpah, his father's wives: and Joseph brought unto his father their evil report.

3   Now Israel loved Joseph more than all his children, because he was the son of his old age: and he made him a coat of many colours.

4   And when his brethren saw that their father loved him more than all his brethren, they hated him, and could not speak peaceably unto him.

5   And Joseph dreamed a dream, and he told it his brethren: and they hated him yet the more.

6   And he said unto them, Hear, I pray you, this dream which I have dreamed:

7   For, behold, we were binding sheaves in the field, and, lo, my sheaf arose, and also stood upright; and, behold, your sheaves stood round about, and made obeisance to my sheaf.

8   And his brethren said to him, Shalt thou indeed reign over us? or shalt thou indeed have dominion over us? And they hated him yet the more for his dreams, and for his words.

9   And he dreamed yet another dream, and told it his brethren, and said, Behold, I have dreamed a dream more;

and, behold, the sun and the moon and the eleven stars made obeisance to me.

10 And he told it to his father, and to his brethren: and his father rebuked him, and said unto him, What is this dream that thou hast dreamed? Shall I and thy mother and thy brethren indeed come to bow down ourselves to thee to the earth?

11 And his brethren envied him; but his father observed the saying.

Overview

Just as our lives have been influenced by countless others, so our lives will influence countless other lives. In this lesson, we learn from the tests Joseph endured throughout his life how to effectively steward our influence to glorify God and bless others.

Introduction

_____

_____

_____

I.   The Test of _____

2 TIMOTHY 3:12

12   Yea, and all that will live godly in Christ Jesus shall suffer persecution.

A.   The _____ *of the dream*

GENESIS 37:6–7, 9

6   And he said unto them, Hear, I pray you, this dream which I have dreamed:

7   For, behold, we were binding sheaves in the field, and, lo, my sheaf arose, and also stood upright; and, behold, your sheaves stood round about, and made obeisance to my sheaf.

9   And he dreamed yet another dream, and told it his brethren, and said, Behold, I have dreamed a dream more; and, behold, the sun and the moon and the eleven stars made obeisance to me.

B.   The _____ *of the dream*

1 THESSALONIANS 2:13

13   For this cause also thank we God without ceasing, because, when ye received the word of God which ye heard of us, ye received it not as the word of men, but as it is in truth, the word of God, which effectually worketh also in you that believe.

1. Envy

GENESIS 37:4, 11

4   And when his brethren saw that their father loved him more than all his brethren, they hated him, and could not speak peaceably unto him.

11   And his brethren envied him; but his father observed the saying.

2. Ridicule

GENESIS 37:19

19   And they said one to another, Behold, this dreamer cometh.

3. Malice

GENESIS 37:20

20   Come now therefore, and let us slay him, and cast him into some pit, and we will say, Some evil beast hath devoured him: and we shall see what will become of his dreams.

II. The Test of _____

GENESIS 39:2–4

2   And the LORD was with Joseph, and he was a prosperous man; and he was in the house of his master the Egyptian.

3   And his master saw that the LORD was with him, and that the LORD made all that he did to prosper in his hand.

4   And Joseph found grace in his sight, and he served him: and he made him overseer over his house, and all that he had he put into his hand.

A. Runs from _____

GENESIS 39:12

12 *And she caught him by his garment, saying, Lie with me: and he left his garment in her hand, and fled, and got him out.*

1 PETER 5:8

8 *Be sober, be vigilant; because your adversary the devil, as a roaring lion, walketh about, seeking whom he may devour.*

JAMES 4:7

7 *Resist the devil, and he will flee from you.*

GENESIS 39:8–10

8 *But he refused, and said unto his master's wife, Behold, my master wotteth not what is with me in the house, and he hath committed all that he hath to my hand;*

9 *There is none greater in this house than I; neither hath he kept back any thing from me but thee, because thou art his wife: how then can I do this great wickedness, and sin against God?*

10 *And it came to pass, as she spake to Joseph day by day, that he hearkened not unto her, to lie by her, or to be with her.*

B. Runs with _____

GENESIS 43:32

32 *…because the Egyptians might not eat bread with the Hebrews; for that is an abomination unto the Egyptians.*

JEREMIAH 9:23–24

23 *Thus saith the LORD, Let not the wise man glory in his wisdom, neither let the mighty man glory in his might, let not the rich man glory in his riches:*

24 But let him that glorieth glory in this, that he understandeth and knoweth me, that I am the LORD which exercise lovingkindness, judgment, and righteousness, in the earth: for in these things I delight, saith the LORD.

III.   The Test of _____

A. Joseph _____ **wrongfully**

GENESIS 39:19–20

19 And it came to pass, when his master heard the words of his wife, which she spake unto him, saying, After this manner did thy servant to me; that his wrath was kindled. 20 And Joseph's master took him, and put him into the prison, a place where the king's prisoners were bound: and he was there in the prison.

GENESIS 39:21

21 But the LORD was with Joseph, and shewed him mercy, and gave him favour in the sight of the keeper of the prison.

B. Joseph _____ **patiently**

GENESIS 40:14–15, 23

14 But think on me when it shall be well with thee, and shew kindness, I pray thee, unto me, and make mention of me unto Pharaoh, and bring me out of this house: 15 For indeed I was stolen away out of the land of the Hebrews: and here also have I done nothing that they should put me into the dungeon. 23 Yet did not the chief butler remember Joseph, but forgat him.

GENESIS 41:14

14   Then Pharaoh sent and called Joseph, and they brought him hastily out of the dungeon: and he shaved himself, and changed his raiment, and came in unto Pharaoh.

IV. The Test of _____

A. He was _____ by God

GENESIS 41:38–39

38   And Pharaoh said unto his servants, Can we find such a one as this is, a man in whom the Spirit of God is?
39   And Pharaoh said unto Joseph, Forasmuch as God hath shewed thee all this, there is none so discreet and wise as thou art.

PSALM 75:6–7

6   For promotion cometh neither from the east, nor from the west, nor from the south.
7   But God is the judge: he putteth down one, and setteth up another.

B. He _____ his prosperity

GENESIS 45:3

3   And Joseph said unto his brethren, I am Joseph; doth my father yet live? And his brethren could not answer him; for they were troubled at his presence.

GENESIS 45:5

5   Now therefore be not grieved, nor angry with yourselves, that ye sold me hither: for God did send me before you to preserve life.

Conclusion

1 CORINTHIANS 4:2

2   Moreover it is required in stewards, that a man be found faithful.

Study Questions

1. How does God reveal Himself to man today?

2. What is the greatest danger in the test of persecution?

3. What caused Joseph to have victory over temptation?

4. When will our influence have the greatest impact for the Lord?

5. Who can you think of that is directly influenced by your life? (Name as many as you can.) Is your influence having a good impact on their life?

6. What boundaries have you set in your life to keep you from giving in to temptation?

7. God wants us to use our faithfulness for His glory. Name a situation in the past week where you used your influence for the glory of God.

8. Influence for God is not won by struggle. It is won by faithfulness. In every area of stewardship, God simply requires faithfulness. Are you faithfully stewarding your influence? Give some examples.

Memory Verses

PSALM 75:6–7

6 *For promotion cometh neither from the east, nor from the west, nor from the south.*

7 *But God is the judge: he putteth down one, and setteth up another.*

Stewarding Testimony

Text

2 TIMOTHY 3:10–15

10   But thou hast fully known my doctrine, manner of life, purpose, faith, longsuffering, charity, patience,

11   Persecutions, afflictions, which came unto me at Antioch, at Iconium, at Lystra; what persecutions I endured: but out of them all the Lord delivered me.

12   Yea, and all that will live godly in Christ Jesus shall suffer persecution.

13   But evil men and seducers shall wax worse and worse, deceiving, and being deceived.

14   But continue thou in the things which thou hast learned and hast been assured of, knowing of whom thou hast learned them;

15   And that from a child thou hast known the holy scriptures, which are able to make thee wise unto salvation through faith which is in Christ Jesus.

Overview

A Christian's testimony goes beyond his salvation story. It is not only about the time and location of his salvation, but it is about his whole life. And a Christian's testimony is not ultimately to leave a legacy for his own name, but rather, for the name of his Saviour, Jesus Christ.

Introduction

_____

_____

_____

ACTS 8:3

3   As for Saul, he made havock of the church, entering into every house, and haling men and women committed them to prison.

ACTS 9:1

1   And Saul, yet breathing out threatenings and slaughter against the disciples of the Lord, went unto the high priest.

2 TIMOTHY 3:10–15

10   But thou hast fully known my doctrine, manner of life, purpose, faith, longsuffering, charity, patience,

11   Persecutions, afflictions, which came unto me at Antioch, at Iconium, at Lystra; what persecutions I endured: but out of them all the Lord delivered me.

12   Yea, and all that will live godly in Christ Jesus shall suffer persecution.

13   But evil men and seducers shall wax worse and worse, deceiving, and being deceived.

14   But continue thou in the things which thou hast learned and hast been assured of, knowing of whom thou hast learned them;

15   And that from a child thou hast known the holy scriptures, which are able to make thee wise unto salvation through faith which is in Christ Jesus.

I. _____ on the _____

2 Timothy 3:10

10 But thou hast fully known my doctrine…

2 Timothy 4:3

3 For the time will come when they will not endure sound doctrine; but after their own lusts shall they heap to themselves teachers, having itching ears;

A. *The doctrine of the* _____

2 Timothy 3:16

16 All scripture is given by inspiration of God, and is profitable for doctrine, for reproof, for correction, for instruction in righteousness.

B. *The doctrine of the* _____

John 10:30

30 I and my Father are one.

Colossians 2:9

9 For in him dwelleth all the fullness of the Godhead bodily.

1 Timothy 3:16

16 And without controversy great is the mystery of godliness: God was manifest in the flesh, justified in the Spirit, seen of angels, preached unto the Gentiles, believed on in the world, received up into glory.

1. Jesus is the Creator of the world

Colossians 1:16

16 For by him were all things created, that are in heaven, and that are in earth, visible and invisible, whether they be thrones, or dominions, or principalities, or powers: all things were created by him, and for him

2. Jesus received worship as God

JOHN 20:28
28 And Thomas answered and said unto him, My Lord and my God.

3. Jesus forgave sin as God

MARK 2:5
5 When Jesus saw their faith, he said unto the sick of the palsy, Son, thy sins be forgiven thee.

4. Jesus is unchanging (immutable) like God

HEBREWS 13:8
8 Jesus Christ the same yesterday, and to day, and for ever.

II. _____ Your _____

A. A life of _____

2 TIMOTHY 3:10
10 But thou hast fully known my doctrine, manner of life, purpose, faith, longsuffering, charity, patience

2 CORINTHIANS 5:17
17 Therefore if any man be in Christ, he is a new creature: old things are passed away; behold, all things are become new.

1 TIMOTHY 3:9
9 *Holding the mystery of the faith in a pure conscience*

PHILIPPIANS 1:27
27 *Only let your conversation be as it becometh the gospel of Christ: that whether I come and see you, or else be absent, I may hear of your affairs, that ye stand fast in one spirit, with one mind striving together for the faith of the gospel.*

B. A life of _____

PHILIPPIANS 3:7–8, 10
7 *But what things were gain to me, those I counted loss for Christ.*
8 *Yea doubtless, and I count all things but loss for the excellency of the knowledge of Christ Jesus my Lord: for whom I have suffered the loss of all things, and do count them but dung, that I may win Christ,*
10 *That I may know him, and the power of his resurrection, and the fellowship of his sufferings, being made conformable unto his death.*

1. At Corinth

1 CORINTHIANS 9:16
16 *…for necessity is laid upon me; yea, woe is unto me, if I preach not the gospel!*

2. At Thessalonica

ACTS 17:2–3
2 *And Paul, as his manner was, went in unto them, and three sabbath days reasoned with them out of the scriptures,*

3   Opening and alleging, that Christ must needs have suffered, and risen again from the dead; and that this Jesus, whom I preach unto you, is Christ.

3. At Ephesus

ACTS 20:20–21

20   And how I kept back nothing that was profitable unto you, but have shewed you, and have taught you publickly, and from house to house,
21   Testifying both to the Jews, and also to the Greeks, repentance toward God, and faith toward our Lord Jesus Christ.

MARK 16:15

15   Go ye into all the world, and preach the gospel to every creature.

III. _____ Your _____

A. *Persevering in* _____

2 TIMOTHY 3:11

11   Persecutions, afflictions, which came unto me at Antioch, at Iconium, at Lystra; what persecutions I endured: but out of them all the Lord delivered me.

ACTS 13:50

50   But the Jews stirred up the devout and honourable women, and the chief men of the city, and raised persecution against Paul and Barnabas, and expelled them out of their coasts.

Acts 14:2, 5–7

2 But the unbelieving Jews stirred up the Gentiles, and made their minds evil affected against the brethren.

5 And when there was an assault made both of the Gentiles, and also of the Jews with their rulers, to use them despitefully, and to stone them,

6 They were ware of it, and fled unto Lystra and Derbe, cities of Lycaonia, and unto the region that lieth round about:

7 And there they preached the gospel.

Acts 14:19–20

19 And there came thither certain Jews from Antioch and Iconium, who persuaded the people, and, having stoned Paul, drew him out of the city, supposing he had been dead.

20 Howbeit, as the disciples stood round about him, he rose up, and came into the city: and the next day he departed with Barnabas to Derbe.

Acts 14:21

21 And when they had preached the gospel to that city, and had taught many, they returned again to Lystra, and to Iconium, and Antioch,

2 Timothy 3:12

12 Yea, and all that will live godly in Christ Jesus shall suffer persecution.

B. Persevering in _____

2 Timothy 3:14

14 But continue thou in the things which thou hast learned and hast been assured of, knowing of whom thou hast learned them.

Conclusion

Study Questions

1. What is the most important question in relation to our testimony?

2. What was the last book of the Bible written by Paul, and from where did he write it?

3. When Paul wrote to Timothy about his testimony, what did he speak of first?

4. What two areas of doctrine are especially important for Christians to believe?

5. In what specific ways does your testimony bring (or not bring) honor to your Saviour?

6. God's Word is profitable to our lives. What changes has it initiated in your life? What profit have you experienced from those changes?

7. Paul's simple life purpose statement would be "To know Christ and to make Him known." Take some time, and, asking the Lord for guidance, write out a personal life purpose statement.

8. Write about a situation in which you have suffered persecution because of your walk with the Lord.

Memory Verse

PROVERBS 22:1

1 *A good name is rather to be chosen than great riches, and loving favour rather than silver and gold.*

Stewarding the Gospel

Text

MARK 16:15

15 *Go ye into all the world, and preach the gospel to every creature.*

1 CORINTHIANS 15:3–4

3 *For I delivered unto you first of all that which I also received, how that Christ died for our sins according to the scriptures;*
4 *And that he was buried, and that he rose again the third day according to the scriptures.*

Overview

Christ's final command before He left Earth was for us to go into all the world and take the gospel to everyone. Stewarding the gospel is a command for every Christian. In this final lesson of Stewarding Life we will look at not only Christ's command to steward the gospel, but also at some testimonies of others who have shared the gospel and the fruit that resulted.

Introduction

_____

_____

_____

JOHN 8:32
32 *And ye shall know the truth, and the truth shall make you free.*

MARK 8:35
35 *For whosoever will save his life shall lose it; but whosoever shall lose his life for my sake and the gospel's, the same shall save it.*

I. His _____ Is Our _____

MARK 16:15
15 *Go ye into all the world, and preach the gospel to every creature.*

1 CORINTHIANS 15:3–4
3   *For I delivered unto you first of all that which I also received, how that Christ died for our sins according to the scriptures;*
4   *And that he was buried, and that he rose again the third day according to the scriptures.*

LUKE 15:4–5
4   *What man of you, having an hundred sheep, if he lose one of them, doth not leave the ninety and nine in the wilderness, and go after that which is lost, until he find it?*
5   *And when he hath found it, he layeth it on his shoulders, rejoicing.*

II. The _____ Is a _____

1 THESSALONIANS 2:4

4   But as we were allowed of God to be put in trust with the gospel, even so we speak; not as pleasing men, but God, which trieth our hearts.

2 CORINTHIANS 5:19

19   To wit, that God was in Christ, reconciling the world unto himself, not imputing their trespasses unto them; and hath committed unto us the word of reconciliation.

LUKE 15:10

10   Likewise, I say unto you, there is joy in the presence of the angels of God over one sinner that repenteth.

III. _____ Is an

_____

PROVERBS 11:30

30   The fruit of the righteous is a tree of life; and he that winneth souls is wise.

A. A _____ investment

B. A _____ investment

ACTS 1:8

8   But ye shall receive power, after that the Holy Ghost is come upon you: and ye shall be witnesses unto me both in Jerusalem, and in all Judaea, and in Samaria, and unto the uttermost part of the earth.

JOHN 16:8

8   *And when he is come, he will reprove the world of sin, and of righteousness, and of judgment.*

- **They pray for a burden.**

REVELATION 20:15

15   *And whosoever was not found written in the book of life was cast into the lake of fire.*

1 PETER 1:3–5

3   *Blessed be the God and Father of our Lord Jesus Christ, which according to his abundant mercy hath begotten us again unto a lively hope by the resurrection of Jesus Christ from the dead,*

4   *To an inheritance incorruptible, and undefiled, and that fadeth not away, reserved in heaven for you,*

5   *Who are kept by the power of God through faith unto salvation ready to be revealed in the last time.*

MATTHEW 9:36

36   *But when he saw the multitudes, he was moved with compassion on them, because they fainted, and were scattered abroad, as sheep having no shepherd.*

- **They carry gospel tracts.**

- **They schedule time for soulwinning.**

- **They keep an updated prospect list.**

- **They are attentive in church services.**

- **They demonstrate hospitality.**

- **They involve new converts in soulwinning.**

JOHN 16:8–9

8   *And when he is come, he will reprove the world of sin, and of righteousness, and of judgment:*

9   *Of sin, because they believe not on me;*

Conclusion

1 CORINTHIANS 4:1–2

1   *Let a man so account of us, as of the ministers of Christ, and stewards of the mysteries of God.*

2   *Moreover it is required in stewards, that a man be found faithful.*

_____

_____

_____

Study Questions

1. Mark 16:15 records Christ's final command before He ascended to Heaven. What is that command?

2. What characteristic does Proverbs 11:30 use to describe the soulwinner?

3. According to Acts 1:8 and John 16:8, who empowers us as soulwinners as well as convicts the lost of their need for Christ?

4. When Paul penned 1 Corinthians 4:2, *"Moreover it is required in stewards, that a man be found faithful,"* to what specific stewardship was he referring?

5. Realistically, where does Christ's last command rank in your list of priorities? To what degree have you made His last command your first priority?

6. Carrying gospel tracts helps us to be soul conscious wherever we go. Check your pockets/purse right now—do you have tracts? If not, purpose to begin carrying them today.

7. Do you participate in your church's regularly scheduled soulwinning program? If not, can you carve out time in your schedule to participate, or is there an alternate time you can carve out weekly to go soulwinning with a partner? This is a perfect time to make yourself accountable to insure that you will go.

8. When was the last time you have shown hospitality to unsaved person, enabling you to share the gospel with them?

Memory Verse

MARK 16:15
15 *Go ye into all the world, and preach the gospel to every creature.*

For additional Christian
growth resources visit
strivingtogether.com